Messages

Behind the Melodies

Songs for Life

Written By:
J.C. White
with Kenyon R. Dudley

Scripture quotations are taken from the *Holy Bible*, New Living Translation, copyright ©1996, 2004, 2007 by Tyndale House Foundation; the *Holy Bible,* King James Version. New York: American Bible Society: 1999 Holy Bible, King James Version, copyright © 1999 by New York: Bible Society; and the *Holy Bible,* Amplified Version, *Copyright © 2015.*

Printed in the United States of America

THIS BOOK IS NOT INTENDED TO BE A HISTORY TEXT. While every effort has been made to check the accuracy of dates, locations, and historical information, no claims are made as to the accuracy of such information.

For book orders, author appearance inquires and interviews, contact author. Contact information at the back of this book.

ISBN-13: 978-0998802565

ISBN-10: 0998802565

Dudley Publishing House

DEDICATIONS

Book dedication is in memory of my mother Annie Mae White, my father James Alfred White, my uncles Bishop Carl E. Williams Sr. and Bishop Jasper J. Williams Jr., and my mother-in-law Mother Eliese Leaphart. These were some of the most influential Saints in my life. They—without a doubt—showed me that if you believe, nothing is impossible, and that God's strength is perfect in your weakness. They used what they had when what they had seemed like nothing at all. Through their lives, I've witnessed little become much. Their faith was always at work. They supported every single effort that I put forth from beginning to end. They believed in me, trusted in me, but most importantly they gave me Godly guidance and prayed for me. To my ancestors, this one is for you.

$\mathcal{T}$HANK YOU TO MY GLO!

I appreciate and love God's gift to me, my lovely, vivacious wife who has been the epitome of the word *helpmate.*

Gloria—who I affectionately call *Glo*—has been by my side through fifty-eight years. She has been deeply active in my book with suggestions, writing, phrasing and pushing me to the finish line. I couldn't have done this project without her input.

Gloria has also sung a great number of my songs that both the Institutional Radio Choir and the J.C. White Singers recorded. Back in the 50's was a part of a group called *The Tones of Glory* who sang one of the first professionally recorded songs that I wrote. She also sung so many that were not published.

I can't express the gratitude I owe her for all that she has sacrificed to make me better in every way. To God be the glory, and I can't tell the entire story, for the gift that was perfect for me. She's my glory, my glow, my Glo!

ACKNOWLEDGMENTS

There are so many people who have been instrumental and very helpful to me as I have endeavored to share the gospel in word and song.

First of all, I would like to thank God Almighty because He gave me these gifts and talents of ministering and writing songs. He anointed them, and has blessed me tremendously to share His great Gospel.

He caused my gift to make room for me. I give all glory and honor to Him.

To my mother and father, who are both with our Father in Heaven. Besides bringing me into the world, they always supported me with words of encouragement and prayer.

I would like to thank my Pastor of 30 years, the late Bishop Carl E. Williams Sr. He was also my biological uncle. Bishop Williams allowed me to minister at home and abroad, trusting me to uphold the Word of God and his good name.

I am especially grateful to my wife Gloria and my children Michon, Steve, Cassandra, Javon and Trina for being so patient and self-sacrificing through the years.

Thank you to Tracey Criss, our church administrator, for her untiring and excellent work. She has helped me in every area of ministry. I am more than grateful.

Thank you to my personal publicist and my nephew, Kesean Joseph, for his contribution to this project.

To each one of the leaders and background

singers of both the Institutional Radio Choir who gave us their time and talents over the decades. It would be another book if I named them one by one.

I must say Thank You to my siblings, Alfred White, Beverly Walker, Lillian Dominick, O' Brian White and Tyrita Williams who were with me from the very beginning and have allowed me to test my writing skills on them through the years.

I would also like to thank The JC White Singers. First, I thank our dedicated and God-appointed Manager, Robert Johnson and his graceful wife, Eloise Johnson. I would also like to thank the singers: Doris "Dot" White-Zitowitz, Gail Graham *(my niece)*, Betty Campbell, Brenda Harrison, Lynda Wilkerson, Irene Wilson, Margaret Grace, Carolyn Johnson White, Bishop Eric and Lady Doreen Figueroa, Angela Washington, and

Arlene Lomax.

Pastor John and Lady Rubinstein McClure, Janet White, Alvin White, Walter Dixon, Melvin Johnson, Eddie Harper and Fredericka LaFleur; and to the late Janet Napper, Joyce Taylor, Deloris Phillips, Pastor Martin Chapman and Jimmy Triplet.

I would also like to thank those who gave me opportunities and exposure: Pastor Shirley Caesar, Milton Biggham, Pastor T.L. Rogers the late world-famous jazz artist, Max Roach, and to the many churches and pastors around the country who have invited us to minister. I take none of this for granted. I thank you a million times over.

$\mathcal{OS}$ONG SOLOIST
ACKNOWLEDGMENTS

I'm often asked, "How did you choose leaders for the songs you wrote?" I usually heard the voice of the leader singing it as I wrote it. I've been told many times that the person I heard was the perfect one. I'd like to call that being in tune with the spirit of God. He's the one who revealed their voices to me as I wrote. The tonality, attitude and personality of the person leading the song played a large part in its effectiveness. For instance, Rubinstein McClure came to us from Birmingham, Alabama where she had been exposed to strict holiness and carried a no-nonsense kind of persona. Don't get me wrong though, she loves to laugh and have fun. In fact, my wife and I like being in the company of her and her husband because of their love for fun, but it's amazing when this woman gets the microphone in her hand. The sincerity of her relationship with God always comes through. She's still singing, to this day, with that same fervor, with that serious face, and with a voice that says, "You better hear me. I know what I'm talking about. When in doubt or in despair, anytime, anywhere, talk it over with Jesus." Ha! Her knowledge of the truth that there is one who understands our hearts continues to keep her reminding others that it's *No One but Jesus.*

Maxine Jones was indeed a precious soul. She led the song *Satisfied with Jesus.* There was a certain softness to her voice that was brought over from her experience with singing hymns in her former church in Virginia. Bishop Williams loved playing the piano and having her sing. Sometimes on Sundays, after church, they would get together around the piano between services and serenade whomever was sitting around waiting. It was kind of unorthodox to have her lead a fast song, but she's who I heard and she mastered it. She's with the Lord now but I would like to thank her family for loaning her to us. She was a tremendous blessing to the choir.

The late renowned and acclaimed Joyce Taylor led many songs and we never left a concert that she had not gained a few new friends. She was so touchable. She possessed a unique voice that she developed herself by faith in God that she could do it. Her faith in God and her love for people made

"Can't Let A Day Go By" the right song for her.

She certainly did have a testimony of how the Lord

provided, protected and directed her as she endured

the trials of raising her children and remaining

faithful to God and the church. If she had written a

book of her life it would surely have been a good

read. She was a faithful witness for the Lord, and

the fact that she was, gave brightness to the song

"Can't Let A Day Go By Without Saying

Something For The Lord."

I felt the song "A Little More Grace" needed

that boldness that Delores Phillips had to give it.

She didn't mind expressing what she felt. It takes

humility and boldness at the same time to admit that

you need more and ask for more of what you need.

We've all been there. Delores would set her head to

the side and ask the Lord to give it to her, just like He said He would. She too is in Heaven now, I'd like her son, my grandson, Melvin (Munce) Phillips Jr. to know that his mom is very much missed and that the entire Institutional Family will never forget her faithful service and triumphant stance.

Table Of

Contents

ℬOOK PRAISE

In a world of fleeting, disingenuous relationships, I have a brother who has remained my brother for more than forty years. It has been suggested, if a man in his lifetime has three genuine friends he is truly blessed. John Carlton White is one of my three. A brother like J.C. White does not come in bunches, as grapes do but he is like an apple, they only come one at a time.

It is this brother who has given us songs in which its lyrics tell us a story of life's journeys, of life's struggles and life's victories. Over the years we have heard the message in the songs he has written but now we are blessed to know the message behind the songs.

So just as the Old Testament book of 1 Chronicles captures the back story of many of the Psalms of David, now we have the back story of JC White's songs captured in "The Chronicles of Bishop J.C. White."

T. L. Rogers

Timeless, classic, soulful, powerful and anointed. A few words to describe the compositions of gospel songwriter/arranger John Carlton White, affectionately known as J.C.!

Spanning over six decades and more than 100 original writings J.C. White certainly is the

"Architect of the Modern Church Choir." Such classics as *One More Day*, *I Feel the Spirit Moving*, *A Little More Grace*, *Look Up and See God*, *Keys to the Kingdom*, *You Can Make It*, and *Believe* have echoed through the walls of churches across America.

It was in the 1960's, when this prolific songwriter lent one of his gifts to gospel star Shirley Caesar's album. The song *Stretch Out* delivered by his wife and muse Gloria *(who can sing a song with the soul and drive of Ruth Davis and the wondrous simplicity of Sarah Vaugh)* became and remains a gospel classic.

Covered by choirs all over the world *Stretch Out* catapulted J.C. White into the gospel stratosphere.

Never had we heard a song driven by the bass pedal, drums, and a choir clapping in sync at such record speed. *Stretch Out* revolutionized the choir format as well as the praise and dance experience in the church.

Not becoming a one-hit-wonder, more incredible musical offerings followed.
This is the Right Time, Anytime and Anywhere, and *Talk It Over with Jesus.*
While a gospel composer J.C.'s creations married components of jazz *(Because of You Lord)*, dance music *(Can't Let a Day Go By),* classical *(I Surrender All),* and even revealed an intimate sound in gospel *(When He Touched Me)*, a tour de force performance by Mamie Williams!

A much sought after writer, producer, pianist, choir master, teacher and singer J.C .went on to collaborate with such notables as Max Roach and Edwin and Walter Hawkins.

His expressions have been recorded by The Hempstead Community Choir, J.W. Woody Ensemble, The J.C. White Singers and his premier vehicle the Institutional Radio Choir, dubbed the *hit makers* due to a string of J.C. White successes.

Not only America, but the songs of J.C. White have had global impact. I've had the pleasure to teach and perform these master pieces in Tokyo, Africa, Australia, Paris, Italy, Germany, England, the Carnegie Hall, the Apollo, countless churches and venues.

What is the true testament of a gifted song writer? If it is standing the test of time. The songs of J.C. White would be the premier example of this. They are still being recorded by and influencing today's newer artist.

Ricky Dillard, Hezekiah Walker, James Hall, Fred Hammond, Vickie Winans, T.D. Jakes, Donnie McClurkin, J.J. Hairston, myself and every single choir in the city of Chicago!! We all stand on the shoulders of the Bishop J.C. White.

A writer for the ages!

The songs? Gospel Blessed with Soul!

International Gospel Artist

Dr. Richard Hartley

$\mathcal{F}$OREWORD

I truly believe that the ministry of the choir is the fire behind good Gospel music. Bishop J.C. White and the Institutional Radio Choir birthed one of the most unique *East Coast* Gospel Choir sounds. It was a hard-driving sound that was fast and set your feet on fire. I used to teach his song *Stretch Out* to many choirs across the nation.

His music always had the ability to take you into a high praise. It's important to know that in order to be as effective as Bishop White is in music, you have to live the life that you sing about. He's an amazing songwriter and I remember hearing his music every day everywhere! I knew that *any* of Bishop White's songs that I taught to *any* choir was going to be a good selection.

As a fellow accomplished songwriter, it's easy to say that you sometimes put pressure on yourself. You want to produce new music that your audience love as much as—if not more than—your previous hit. You want to keep the momentum in supplying what your audience wants to hear.

Bishop White was always able to produce hit after hit and bless people around the world. I always say, it's the anointing and a prayer life that enable your music and your sound to stay alive and resound over the years. Both are quite apparent in

Bishop White's ministry today – from music to preaching. That is such a blessing.

Elbernita "Twinkie" Clark

American Gospel singer, composer, musician, evangelist, member of the Hammond organ Hall of Fame, and member of The Clark Sisters

Introduction
Messages
Behind the Melodies

At the age of ten I got my first taste of writing

gospel music. A young lady by the name of Shirley

Hagler wrote what we called church songs and

played the first organ at *First Church*. That was the

church that our family were members of before my

uncle, Bishop Williams, started to Pastor. I was

impressed by her ability. And since I was already

writing poetry, I tried my hand at writing songs.

They were just melodies that I sang to myself and

sometimes tested them out on my sisters and

brothers. After meeting my wife-to-be—and she

being a member of a gospel group—I wrote the first

of my songs to be recorded. By this time, we were

members of the *Institutional Church of God in Christ*. My uncle allowed me to direct the young adult choir. Soon we went on the air, broadcasting every Sunday night at 10:30. That broadcast became very popular. People would come from all over the tri-state to be a part of the service. Our first recording was done by our radio broadcast engineer. I don't even know if it was sold to anyone except the church members. Ha!

Then there came a time when Shirley Caesar wanted a choir to sing background for one of her projects. She came to hear us and decided to use us. She allowed us to put one of our songs on that album. That song was *Stretch Out*. It got lots of air play and our popularity grew fast. All praises to God!

I am very grateful that the Lord used us through the years to encourage and bless others with what He gave us. I am humbled by what God has allowed me to accomplish not only in songs but in the preaching of the gospel of Jesus Christ. I owe everything to Him.

As I wrote songs I had no idea that they would be such a blessing or remembered by so many but I believe the reason that they are is because of the scriptural content. The Word of God is full of power and it will never fail. The grass withered, the flower fadeth: but the word of our God shall stand for ever. (Isaiah 40:8.) If you want something to last be sure that the Word of God is backing it.

I believe that there's meaning to the songs God has given me to write. I've been blessed to be a Gospel artist and writer for decades now. Trust me, it's not all glitz and glamour. Along the way I have learned the essence of who God is, and the power that He possess. I mean this when I say, "I found God in my songwriting career."

I can remember, I asked the Lord a long time ago for songs to be written through me that would impact the lives of my generation and the lives of generations to come. I wanted more during that time. I wanted more of God. Although I was called into ministry, I have always had this knack for writing songs.

I recognized the call on my life to preach and teach the Word of God and have been Pastoring the wonderful people of God at the same church, *Cathedral of Praise*, for almost 38 years now. I believe that my foundation of writing and singing gospel songs drew to my ministry some of the finest, anointed and gifted singers in the world.

Back in the day, we traveled all over the country. We had some good times and wonderful times on those tours. We stopped in St. Louis, Chicago, and other cities on the way from New York to California ministering the Word of God in song. Those were the days.

On the tour of 1969 we met up with another choir, who was traveling also. They were *The Star*

of Bethlehem COGIC Choir of Washington, DC.
Harvey Lewis, the choir's director and songwriter, was like a role model to me. We admired each other's music and I was happy to see him, but that was a day that I remember for another reason. That was the day that we met T. L. Rogers whom I now refer to as my *"brother from another mother."* The only two seats left in the restaurant where we stopped to eat was at the table where Gloria—my wife—and I was seated. Tommy and his wife Mable took those two seats that day and the rest is history. We were friends for life.

We arrived in California where we did a concert and after it was over Andrae Crouch and the Hawkins brothers—Walter and Edwin Hawkins— met us back stage. We chatted for a while and started to say our good byes, but that's when Andrae invited us to spend the night at his house. We felt so honored, we went back by the hotel, picked up some clothes and went over to his place. Ha! That's when I discovered that Andrae *loved* bacon, eggs and jelly sandwiches. That was a little odd to some. But when I think about it now I can see that this was his way of showing that he was out-of-the-box. He always kicked against the norm; which he certainly showed us through his music. He was not afraid to put out there what he produced even though it was not the normal traditional Gospel music of the time. He stepped out-of-the-box and crossed cultural lines. That was just his standard. I'm grateful to have met and become good friends with the legendary Andrae Crouch.

We ate, talked and he played music until the wee hours of the morning the night of our stay at Andrae's place. That night, Andrae gave me little wisdom tidbits like, "Get all of your music copyrighted." I immediately went back home and signed up with BMI.

I revered Andrae Crouch because he was delivering a different sound back in the day. His songs were crossovers. I mean, he had the white audience as well as the black audience. All of the aspiring gospel artists looked to Andrae Crouch. He was our trail blazer in the Gospel music arena. There's no doubt, his style influenced my writing for the *J.C. White Singers.*

During those times, I can remember Joe Bostic Jr., New York's Gospel most popular music disc jockey. He called us the *Hit Makers* back then. Wow! We had so many good songs during that time. But I had help writing and producing all this music. A great number of them were written by Butch Heyward—one of the meekest, talented and admired men I know—and other songs were arranged by John Hason as well. John was an amazing arranger from California who played piano for the world-renowned Gospel writer and singer James Cleveland. Together, we recorded thirty albums between the *Institutional Radio Choir and the J. C. White Singers.*

As the years passed, we went on recording. For the longest I was a Choir Director. I had heard mostly quartets and I wanted to be different. I wanted to write *Gospel* music, which is very different from quartet music. Back then it was quartets, then choirs came along. I was of the choir age.

My choir travelled around Chicago, New York, DC, and other cities around the country for several years. But we never travelled to the south. So they called us the *Hitmakers of the Northeast.* Mr. Joe Bostic was a disc jockey who was on the air every morning and Saturdays all day. His son was the one who named us *The Hitmakers*, 170 Delphi Street. Ha! Oh my goodness, those were the days.

I was signed to United Artists in the 60s. They hired me to write songs for some of the label's top artists. God was smiling upon me. I've always loved writing songs and my dreams were coming into full manifestation as I became one of the writers for United Artist Record Label. One weekend I went to Youth Congress in Texas. I was inundated with my writing at the time. After the Congress was over I left my songbook. I called back to a friend who—at the time—sang with the Stars of Faith. She found my briefcase and said she was coming to New York soon because the Stars were booked to sing at the Apollo. I was to meet her there in the backstage of the Apollo to get my book. If you don't know by now, my songbook was my life. When I had left it in Texas I didn't know what I was going to do. All the songs that I had written for the artists over at United were in there.

You could imagine I was going to travel far and wide just to get that book back.

So, a few weeks later I showed up at the Apollo. When I went backstage my friend let me know that she had left my songbook in her car. I immediately went to 126th Street to her car to get it. When I got there, I found that someone had broken into her car and taken my book. I was so devastated. I couldn't even remember the words from any of the forty plus songs I had written. I was depressed for a little more than two months. I mean, *really* depressed. I couldn't shake it. Why would God allow something like this to happen to me? At the time, I was already married, but I wasn't any good to my wife. All I could do was question God. I felt as if I lost time. And yes, I had. Ultimately, I was unable to get the music to the company and I was eventually let go from United Artists. There it was; another hard blow of reality.

Soon, I got my determination back. I began to write again. I told the Lord, "If you give me songs with meaning, I'll dedicate these songs to you. I will give them back to you again

In 1975, during the height of my songwriting career, I was promoted to an Elder in the Lord's church. In 1979, I was sent to Connecticut to pastor a church called *Turners Faith Temple*. In 2008 we changed the name of the church to *Cathedral of Praise*. When I was first sent out to pastor, I told the Lord, "I'll Pastor, but I still want to write songs." I can still remember bargaining with Him. At certain times, God would still give me songs, but ultimately, I started putting ministry and preaching first. For years, I tried and tried to come up with sermons from the messages behind the songs I wrote. And for years I was unable to do so. But I never gave up hope, and now here I am. I'm writing this book of messages and lessons I've learned along the way. And the messages come directly from many of the songs I've been blessed to write.

I believe that now is the time. Right now, I have a release in my spirit. I hope you will enjoy *the messages behind the melodies*, but most of all gain some scriptural knowledge and encouragement to live whole-heartedly for the Lord. Jesus is coming!

My wife was the lead on the song *Stretch Out,
Keys to the Kingdom, It's Mighty Nice to Be A
Witness for The Lord, You Can Make It, This Is the
Answer* and many others. Our closing song for
every concert for a long while was *Stretch Out*.
That's the song that the choir was most known for.
The audience was always left shouting, dancing,
praising and worshiping the Lord. Why that song I
don't know, but I'm grateful.

After leaving New York and the
Institutional Church we would go back from time to
time. We were very well received and it brought us
joy to sing and fellowship with the brothers and
sisters that we grew up with, toured the country
with, laughed and yes sometimes even cried

with. I salute all of them. Many of them are no longer with us, but their service and dedication will always be remembered.

A couple of years ago I went to London, England and was asked to preach in three different cities. I was pleasantly surprised to find out that many pastors knew of my music and expressed their desire to see it come back. They reverenced the messages in the songs and how it made them feel. My prayer is that these messages will now translate to a new generation. I pray that the messages I reveal in this book would cause you to gain more knowledge and understanding of who God really is and how much He wants to commune with you. *As you read this book and sing these songs enjoy the melodies while absorbing the message.*

1

Stretch Out - 1966

Many of the songs I wrote are inspired and heavily drenched in the revelation of my spiritual father and pastor. Boy, the sermons and messages that this man would preach were always on fire. I was often captivated by them. I can still remember when God gave me the song *Stretch Out* to write. It came from a message that my pastor preached.

Now, I'll be honest, I didn't quite understand in totality just what the phrase *stretch out* meant back then, but as life continued I soon understood. Stretching out isn't just some cute colloquialism that I came up with. It's not just some fancy clever hook in a song that was written to get the masses up and out of their seats. No, stretching out literally means stretching out on the word of God.

You've got to have met some rough and hard times to know what I mean. Have you ever experienced some bad news that just made you fall to your knees? Have you ever received a report that wasn't in your favor, and no one else could handle it but God? See, life has its way of bringing you into rough and arduous places; places where you can't do anything but lean and depend on the Almighty God. These are those times and moments where you learn to stretch out on what God says in His word. These are the moments where you must go to God in prayer and remind him of His promises to you.

For decades now, my wife—and many others like the great Shirley Caesar and Vickie Winans—have sung this song with so much conviction. I believe it's because they too have had their own share of ups and downs and challenges. They too know something about the power of stretching out in faith; believing God's Word no matter what your going through.

What will you do? You may be going through a difficult season in your life right now. Is something troubling you right now? Some of the best advice I can give you is, "Learn how to stretch out on the promises of God."

Know that God is with you because He promised that He would never leave you. Know that if you pray according to His will He hears you, and if He hears you then you can know that you have the petitions that you ask of Him (1 John 5:14-15). Our job is to pray to Him according to His Word. If He promised it in His Word, then He wants you to have it. No good thing will He withhold from the ones who walk upright before Him. Psalms 84:11 says it. Put your trust in that. Stretch out on that Word and receive your answer. Some might think that this Psalm is saying you must be perfect to get the good things that God is talking about, but oh no. A child of God *is* the righteous. The righteous are already in right standing with God. We are not perfect but because we are in Christ, God looks at us through Christ and sees us *as* perfect. Therefore, we can accept whatever good things we desire according to His will.

The blessing is in the stretching. Stretching is believing the impossible. Stretching is calling those things that be not as though they were. Stretching is standing up on His Word with crippled legs. In Acts 14:10, when Paul perceived that the man had faith to be healed, he said with a loud voice, "Stand up on your feet." And he leaped and walked. Stretching is sticking out a withered arm. Luke 6:10 says, "And looking round about upon them all, He said unto the man, 'Stretch forth thy hand,' and he did so; and his hand was restored whole as the other. Stretching is saying I am strong, when you feel as weak as water. Joel 3:10 says, "beat your plowshares into swords, and your pruninghooks into spears: let the weak say I am strong." Stretching is while in the deepest poverty saying, "I am rich."

You can reach stuff that is higher than you when you stretch out. The world sees your circumstances and think you will never reach your goal, but if you are in Him you have a plus factor; and that is the Word of God. Stretch out on the Word and get your victory!

Esther is a perfect example of stretching out on the Word of God. She saved an entire nation by trusting in His Word. Stretching out on God's instructions given to her by her cousin Mordecai. It indeed was a stretch. She could have lost her life, but she went forth in obedience. The end was *VICTORY*. Just read the book of Esther.

So, when troubles come, and storms begin to rise hold on to your faith and stretch out on God's Word.

Stretch Out
(Led by Lady Gloria White)

When troubles come and storm begins to rise
Hold on and learn to stretch out
Oh keep on trusting keep on believing
Hold on and learn to stretch out

When Satan gets on your track
And tries to turn me back
I won't worry, I won't fret I just stretch out
(Stretch out, oh stretch out)

When days are dark and cloudy are my skies
I hold on and learn to stretch out
Oh keep on fasting, keep on believing
Hold on and learn to

Stretch out

Cause the race isn't given to the swift
Neither is it given to the strong
But to him that endureth to the end
Stretch out, oh stretch out

When I am lonely, when I am sad
Jesus is there to make me glad
There to receive you
The lord won't deceive you

Stretch out
Stretch out
Stretch out on his word

2

Keys to The Kingdom – 1972

Matthew 16:19 says, "I will give you the _keys of the Kingdom_ of the heavens, and whatever you may bind on earth will already be bound in the heavens, and whatever you may loosen on earth will already be loosened in the heavens." Can I tell you that the more years I live on this earth, the more I have come to understand the essence of what this scripture is saying? Do you not know that you have power and authority from God Almighty to access the Kingdom of God?

Keys to the Kingdom was another song about the power and authority we had in Christ, and I just couldn't let it go. The thought of me having direct influence on the heavens and the earth just by the mere power and authority God has given me through His Son Jesus; that just did something to me. It still does.

God has given us one of the greatest weapons known to man. That is our tongue. I'm sure you've heard that life and death are in the tongue. Don't you know that whatever you say all Heaven and earth will back you up?

Over the years, I've learned this principle. That's why I try to watch what I say. Whatever I say is literally giving command to the Heavens and the earth. And let me tell you; they both respond every time.

We have been given keys to the Kingdom. All that means is, we've been given power and authority as children of God to access levels, realms, doors, portals, and even dimensions that we've never seen before. How do you think Joshua in Joshua 10 commanded and caused the sun to stand still while he was in battle? He commanded that it stood still until he won the victory over his enemy. Did you catch that? Joshua commanded and all of Heaven and earth responded in his favor. Why? Because Joshua knew who he was in the Kingdom of God. Joshua knew exactly what He was capable of with the assistance of the Holy Spirit and the power of God.

Now the question is, "Do you?" I wrote songs like, *Keys to the Kingdom,* to drive the point home that you don't have to live a defeated life. If you are saved and have been adopted into the family of God, you no longer have to suffer at the hands and mercy of an enemy that doesn't even hold as much power as you do. You have been granted the keys to success, the keys to wealth, the keys to good health and a sound mind, and so much more.

If there's nothing else that I've learned in life, it's that heavenly forces and earthly forces combined will beckon at the command of person who knows where their help comes from. Psalm 121: 1-2 says, "I will lift up mine eyes unto the hills, from whence cometh my help. My help cometh from the Lord, which made heaven and earth."

Remember God is looking for you to show His strength. 2 Chronicles 16:9 says, "For the eyes of the LORD run to and fro throughout the whole earth, to shew himself strong in the behalf of *them* whose heart *is* perfect toward him." Thank God for keys. Keys gives you access to places that are not accessible to those who do not have them. God does not want us to suffer the lack of anything that would profit or advance us, but you will have to search. Good and valuable stuff is protected There are things that cannot just be left out for just anyone to take. Everyone doesn't know how to handle the treasures that are laid up for the Children of God, but oh how wonderful it is to know that they are laid up for us and not from us. He has given us the keys to access them. Hallelujah! Matthew 16:19 says, "And I will give unto thee the keys of the kingdom of heaven: and whatsoever thou shalt bind on earth shall be bound in heaven: and whatsoever thou shalt loose on earth shall be loosed in Heaven." Peter was given revelation knowledge of who Jesus was by our Father in Heaven and so Jesus gave to Him the keys to loose and bind. Loosing and binding must be done to put a stop to the enemies plans and bring into fruition God's plan in the earth so that we always win. Those keys were not given only to Peter, but to the entire Body of Christ. There have been numerous times when I had to exercise that power. I remember one incident regarding exercising this power. While preaching at another church one Sunday afternoon, a young lady displayed demonic actions and came against me. I called a prayer line and she came up. When I got to her she began to speak in a man's voice though she was just a 16-year-old girl. The voice growled, and the demonic spirit attacked me knocking me to the floor. This was my first encounter with such a force. I weakly from the floor asked the Saints to bind the devil and they did. The Mother's took charge, just like the praying seasoned Mothers will do when they see one of their own in need of help. They bound the devil and loosed me from that spirt. When I was loosed I laid my hands on that young girl and rebuked the demon spirit, and the Lord set her free. Her and her mother's testimony was that she had been bound since she was 12 years old. She had left their home, but that Sunday she desired to come to church. It just so happened to be the right day for her deliverance. It was the day of her liberation. To my surprise she was the pastor's daughter. The devil does not care who he attacks, but God—in His infinite mercy—will set anyone free.

I hope this helps you to understand that it is not our holiness and righteousness that I'm talking about. It is the holiness and righteousness of God working in us to pull down strong holds. He gives us the keys and access to the Kingdom. And in His Kingdom, we have power and victory over the world and Satan's kingdom!

Lyrics

Keys to the Kingdom
(Led By: Lady Gloria White)

You don't have to be a rich man to make it to the city

You don't have to be a doctor or a lawyer to reach that celestial shore

*I'll tell you what the Lord God wants from you,
cause he wants you to make it through
Be Holy (Holy)
Be righteous (righteous)
For this is the keys to the kingdom (doop)*

*You don't have to be a warrior in this mobilized by man
To receive the reward of eternal life given by God's own hand*

*I'll tell you what the Lord God wants of you,
cause he wants you to make it through
Be Holy (Holy)
Be righteous (righteous)
For this is the keys to the kingdom (doop)*

I want you to befriend all of God's children
Help the feeble as well as the weak
Remembering all that you do for them, blessings
you will reap

Be holy (holy)
Be righteous (righteous)

You must be (Must be)
You got to be (got to be)

Holiness (holiness)
Righteousness (righteousness)

This is the keys to the kingdom

3

I'll Show You the Way - 1980

By now you know that songs are my heart. And all I've ever really wanted to do was write God's heart and relay them to the heart of people. This song, *I'll Show You the Way,* is no different. Ephesians 3:16-19 says, "God would grant you, according to the riches of his glory, to be strengthened with might by his Spirit in the inner man; that Christ may dwell in your hearts by faith; that ye, being rooted and grounded in love, may be able to comprehend with all saints what is the breadth, and length, and depth, and height; And to know the love of Christ, which passeth knowledge, that ye might be filled with all the fulness of God."

In this song it was my every intention to relay to the Body of Christ that we have a Savior who does not just stop by to save you from Hell's fire. He's more than that. We don't just have a God that is concerned about our souls being saved from eternal damnation; but we also have a Savior who desires that you would enjoy life. He wants us to enjoy both down here on earth and when we get to Heaven. It's important to understand that God desires that we have life abundantly. God wants us to remember that there's no life like the one He can give to us!

One of my favorite scriptures is 1 Timothy 6:17, "Command those who are rich in the things of this life not to be proud, but to place their hope, not in such an uncertain thing as riches, but in God, who generously gives us everything for our enjoyment." All we have to do is commit ourselves to living a life for God. He'll show us the way it's done! There are principles in life that God have given us, and if we follow them we are sure to prosper and reign in life.

We don't automatically know how to tap into these principles that will advance us and prosper us, but that's why God promised us that He'll never leave us and that He'll never forsake us. God is always there to show us the way to the better life. For sure there is a way! You are never in a situation that God can't bring you out of, and you are never in a place that God can't get the glory out of.

I'm sure you all remember David in the Bible, the forgotten one, Jessie's youngest son, the lion, bear and giant killer the musician, the King. He said, "Yea though I walk through the valley of the shadow of death, I will fear no evil, for you God, are with me. Who better to have with you—as you go through the good and bad times of life—than the *ALMIGHTY GOD*, creator of Heaven and earth? He's the one who never fails, the one with all power in His hand. And He's looking for someone to show Himself strong in behalf of (2 Chronicles 16). God always wants an opportunity to show up and show out!

This song, *I'll Show You the Way,* hopefully encouraged its listeners to ask the Savior to lead and guide them every day in their walk with Him. It is my prayer that many developed a desire for God to help them be what He would have them to be. The Bible says that we are the head and not the tail, above only and not beneath, able to lend and not borrow. These are things that only God can show us how to manifest in our daily lives.

Exodus 13:21-22 says, "And the LORD went before them by day in a pillar of a cloud, to lead the way; and by night in a pillar of fire, to give them light; He took not away the pillar of the cloud by day, nor the pillar of fire by night, from before the people to go by day and night." In the Old Testament, God led the children of Israel through the wilderness. They knew when to move and when not to because of the pillar of cloud by day and a pillar of fire to give them light by night. Listen my friends, we have the Holy Spirit to guide us by day and we have Him shining through the dark times.

I notice that the scripture says they were led by day and by night. This gives us to know that God leads us not only when it's bright, sunny, and when everything's alright; but also when the night comes. God is with us every step of the way. We have light in the darkness. And that's His word, His joy, His peace, and such. That's the way He leads us. He is in us showing us the way by way of His Holy Spirit. If you're listening and paying attention, He's constantly reminding us of the Word of God which gives us the answers and wisdom that we need to guide us through our wilderness experiences. We should not move until He tells us to. We should be able to see, even in the dark times. For we know that God is always showing His children the way. The day and the night are the same to He who knows all things and sees all things. He knows the end from the beginning, and there's no need for us to worry or fret.

Nehemiah 9:19, "Yet thou in thy manifold mercies forsookest them not in the wilderness: the pillar of the cloud departed not from them by day, to lead them in the way; neither the pillar of fire by night, to shew them light, and the way wherein they should go." My friends, notice the pillar of fire by night not only gave them light to see but also the way to go by night. God does not want us to be stopped by night times in our lives. If He says go when it's night, then just know that He will give you light to see your way.

Here's a principal hidden in the scriptures to help you prosper: Isaiah 1:19, "If ye be willing and obedient, ye shall eat the good of the land: But if ye refuse and rebel, ye shall be devoured with the sword: for the mouth of the LORD hath spoken it." Being willing and obedient has everything to do with eating the good of the land. Remember that. Do what God says and you will get what God has for you.

You can't come upon a problem that God can't solve. You can't experience a burden that God can't lift. You can't ask a question that God does not already have the answer to. There is always a way out of and a way into whatever it is that's needed.

Bishop Carl Williams Sr. my Apostle who's now deceased, used to pray to the Lord often saying, "Lord give us the what, the when, the where, and the how." In the battles that Israel fought they always had to enquire of the Lord so that they would know what and how God wanted to fight. If we want to win we must also enquire of the Lord. The way you went or did in your last fight may not be the way He wants you to go this time.

I heard Him say in my spirit, "I'll show you the way, but you will have to let or allow me to do so." To let Him is to ask Him and then to follow His commands.

When your day is dark He is your light. When fear tries to come in He will renew your courage and show you how to use His resources. His resources are things like prayer, fasting, His Word, using His power and authority in His name. Let Him lead you. God will not drive you, but He will lead you if you want to be led. It is important for God's children to be led by Him. David asked God to lead him for His name sake. Psalms 31:3, "For thou art my rock and my fortress; therefore, for thy name's sake lead me, and guide me."

If we have made it known to the world that God is our rock, our firm foundation, and our fortress, our security, the keeper of our souls then we must allow the Lord to lead us so that we will come to our expected end—our victorious state—so that He

is proven to be who He said He is in our lives.
Genesis 15:1 says, "After these things the word of
the LORD came unto Abram in a vision, saying,
"Fear not, Abram: I am thy shield, and thy
exceeding great reward.'" The world will see that
He indeed is just that if we allow Him to lead
us. Oh yes! He will show you the way, but only if
you let Him.

Lyrics

I'll Show You the Way
(Led by Lady Gloria White)

I'll show you the way if you let me
All you have to do is say the word
If you feel lost and forsaken
I'll pick you up and fill your days with myrrh

I'll show you the way just ask me
I'll be there as soon as you call
I'm willing to bear all your burdens
Just ask me to be your all and all

I'll show you the way if you let me
Just say to me I need you
I'll show you the way if you let me
I'll take you by the hand and lead you

In your darkest night
I'll make your pathway bright
When you're going through
Your courage I'll renew

I'll show you the way if you let me

4

It's God, It's God - 1976

In Genies 1:1-2, light came to be because of darkness. The Bible says, "Darkness covered the atmosphere until God spoke light into existence. Because of the darkness, light was needed. God is the author and source of all that we'll ever need in this life. The air we breathe is essential to all. It is the means by which we have life; not only for man but to all living things. Air gives us the ability to walk, talk, think, and even reason. It's, in essence, a gift from God. The Bible is very clear, God is the Creator and designer of our life and all the things within it that sustains us. Creation by design had to be Divine. Grass could not have grown without God giving seed. All vegetation needs water to grow, so God gave water to the earth in the form of rain. If you're like me, you see God in the birds that fly arrayed in exquisite colors, their ability to fly from north to south and from east to west by their God given instincts. You see thousands of animal species with God-given ability and instincts to survive. These things should convince a real truth seeker that no one other than a superior intelligence and a master creator is responsible for this earth, its inhabitants, and the mechanisms that sustain it.

How anyone could not believe in God is just beyond my comprehension, when all of creation is speaking in the loudest voice possible *IT'S GOD! IT'S GOD!* In essence, that's what the song I wrote *It's God, It's God* is all about. My every intention for writing this song was to communicate to the world that everything that was made on earth, in the universe, and in the spirit is all because of our Almighty God.

All the birds and bees, the oceans and seas, the whole animal kingdom, and most of all mankind gives witness day by day that God is real. It saddens me when this generation acknowledges that there is something out there, but that *something* is whatever you think it is or want it to be. Now-a-days people think this way of thinking is ok. If you want it to be Buddha, Muhammed, a statue made of wood, stone or paper then that's what it will be. It could be an animal, or an object, but I say, *NOOOOOOO A THOUSAND TIMES NO!!!*

It's God Jehovah, God the creator of all things. And I'm a bonafide believer of that. The Sun is not God. God is in the sun because He created the sun. The moon is not God. God is in the moon because He created the moon. When I wake up in the morning and see the sun I don't worship the sun I worship the one who created the sun and that's God. No one or nothing else can be God. There is only one true and living God. The God who spoke and the worlds were framed.

People will even give thanks to nothing at all before they will give thanks to God. I hear it every day. Someone will say I am so thankful, but they won't say to who. They will say you are so lucky, but they won't say you're blessed. Why? Because many believe that being *blessed* is equated to God.

And I'll say, it absolutely is. And if you want to be honest, every waking moment of your life is a divine miracle and genuine blessing. God Almighty is the reason for that.

The people of God should sing from the house top daily *"IT'S GOD, IT'S GOD, AND ONLY GOD. HE IS THE ONLY ONE WHO MADE THE MOUNTAINS AND TREES AND THE RIVERS FLOW OUT TO THE SEA'S!"*

I'll be honest, it's hard to keep this bonafide faith in a generation such as we live in today. This particular song *It's God, It's God* was written decades ago. It was a time where it was easy for many to depend on their faith and recognize that only God could grant them each day of living that they received. With Jim Crow, segregation, and many nations around the world not being privy to the modern technology and creative ideals of today; it was easy to rely on a higher power such as God. Nonetheless, it can be hard today to believe that God is our source, because we've become so dependent upon our own intellect, innovations, and such. How quickly do we forget that it was God who gave us the intellect in the first place.

But if you need a reminder on why we should always recognize God as our source; here you go! Just look around you. Everything was literally made to sustain you and I as humans. God created this world and everything in it so that we might be sustained, thrive, and eventually come to be with

Him throughout eternity. That alone is a humbling idea—and if you can admit it—a blessing.

I admonish whoever is reading this book to believe in God. I know it sounds old school, because many people don't preach and teach salvation anymore. Many books now-a-days only speak about how you can help yourself. And all of that is good in its proper place and context. But the main thing to this life is to come to know Jesus and Father God. For without knowing God, accepting His Son, and being able to acknowledge that we have life in God then we are nothing. Our lives are lifeless. Believing that God is God is the prerequisite to coming to Him and you must come to Him in order to be saved. The Scriptures says in Hebrew 6:11, "But without faith it is impossible to please Him: for he that cometh to God must believe that He is, and that He is a rewarder of them that diligently seek Him.

It is my prayer that the old song I wrote years ago still rings in the hearts that it touched then; but most of all I pray that it touches someone right now. If you don't remember anything else, remember this one thing everything good and perfect that's manifesting in your life *It's God, It's God!*

Lyrics

Its God, Its God
(Led by Yours Truly)

What is it? (That makes the raindrops fall)
What is it? (That makes the grass grow tall)
What is it? (That makes the sun shine bright)
What is it? (That makes the moon light up the night)

It's God, it's God
It's only God (repeat)

When you wake up in the morning, feeling fine
Open up the window to the bright sunshine
Even on the days when you see the rain
It's only preparation for the fields of grain

What is it? (That makes the hatred disappear)
What is it? (That dries a mournful tear)
What is it? (That puts the leaves on the trees)
What is it? (That's in a cool summer breeze)

It's God, it's God
It's only God

5

Can't Let a Day Go By - 1978

Gen. 18:18-19 says, "Since Abraham is destined to become a great and mighty nation, and all the nations of the earth will be blessed through him? For I have known (chosen, acknowledged) him [as My own], so that he may teach *and* command his children and [the sons of] his household after him to keep the way of the Lord by doing what is righteous and just, so that the Lord may bring upon Abraham what He has promised him." It is of the upmost importance that God and his goodness be passed on from one generation to another. We must make it our business to say something for and about the Lord. It is especially important to speak about God to our children and their children. Being a witness is one of our reasonable services unto the Lord.

In the scripture of Genesis 18, the reason God chooses not to keep a secret from Abraham is because he had promised to make of him a great and mighty nation, and God knew him that Abraham would instruct and teach his children and his household about The Lord. God knew that Abraham would teach his family to do the right thing. God knew He could trust Abraham to speak well of Him and pass Him along to his family and decedents. This is why God blessed Him so.

Saying something for the Lord and about the Lord means much more than you know. Who knows who will hear and believe. And who knows if your promise hinges on whether you are willing to share what you know about God. Everyday there is a need to magnify the Lord. He has done more for us than any other. There is no lack of things to say or do for the Lord. He gives us daily bread and we owe it to Him even to tell of His deeds among the people and among our families. Whether it's doing something for Him or speaking of what He's done for us. There is a plethora of truth that we can speak daily!

God wants us to be aware of being a witness for Him so that His Kingdom is expanded. God wants hell empty and Heaven full. "It's not His will that any should perish, but that all would come to repentance." God's Son—Christ—died for the whole world. But it's up to those who already believe to witness of this fact. How else will those in the world hear of and see the goodness of Jesus? We've got to always be a witness!

Slim are the days of evangelism in our world; especially in America. I'm declaring that the message of my song *Can't Let a Day Go By* invade the masses even in this new generation. We've got to get back to not being scared to open up our mouths about the awesome wonders of a gracious Eternal God. We've got to get back to not being afraid to walk in the coffee shop and grocery stores just to witness about our Savior. We've got to get back to the unapologetic stance we took for Christ on school grounds and in the midst of Town Hall meetings. Again, we've got some wonderful modern things going on in America and the world, but without the unadulterated witnessing and belief in God like the old days it's all nothing. See, when you open up your mouth and tell the world about Jesus there's a certain power that is released in the atmosphere and on the earth. The scripture says, "If I be lifted up, I will draw all men." Oh my friends, there's something about when you lift His name up. The sick can be healed. The degenerate can be regenerated. The lifeless can live. The lost can be found.

Do you remember the day you got saved? I'm sure you can say that someone Witnessed to you and you were convinced that Jesus is the way to eternal life. Here's the point, God uses people to witness to other people because faith comes by hearing and the scripture says how can they hear without a preacher. A preacher being someone who proclaims the Word of God and sometimes their personal testimony. If the listener will believe and respond by receiving Christ as his personal savior, then they are saved.

There are times in the service of the Lord, church services in particular, where we are reminded of the goodness of the Lord and we are overcome with the thought of how much God loves us. We're overcome with the thought of how much He's done for us. We ponder—as David in the Bible did—when he asked, "What shall I render unto the Lord for all His benefits?" When writing *Can't Let a Day Go By,* my thoughts were, "God you've been so good, so merciful and kind—like David—what can I give unto you in gratitude and thanks? Then I thought, I can't let a day go by without saying something for the Lord. He's been too good for me not to at least talk about Him and brag on Him. It's the least I can do. He holds me back from things that would destroy me. He picked me up when I fell. I must tell it; and by telling it souls will hear and come to Him.

Listen, anytime is the right time to tell what the Lord has done. Every day is a good day to tell somebody about Jesus. Just think if we would all not let a day go by without saying something for the Lord what a difference it would make. The world would quickly be won for Christ.

During the course of a day we have many opportunities to say something for the Lord. You would be surprised what it means to someone just to hear the words, "God loves you, or "The Lord is good," or "Don't worry, God is going to fix it for you." There are times when I will say to someone, "God bless you," and their face will light up and they will respond by saying, "Thank you," as if those words just made their day. Something as simple as this is being a witness for God and can turn someone's whole world around.

God is good and He needs us to tell of His goodness. Some say they don't know how or what to say. Well the Word of God is a good teacher. Psalms 107:2, "Let the redeemed of the LORD say so, whom he hath redeemed from the hand of the enemy; *tell of Your redemption.* You have been bought with a price, the blood of Jesus was shed to redeem you. You are free and given authority to reign in the earth." Wouldn't everyone want to know who gives this kind of freedom and were to find Him? Verse 15 of that same chapter says, "Oh that men would praise the LORD *for his goodness, and for his wonderful works to the children of men*! Wouldn't it be wonderful if men would tell of the goodness of the Lord? There are plenty of good and awesome things to tell about God.

When we find anything that helps us or gives us joy we usually tell our friends and neighbors about it. Why not tell them about the Good God that loves us with an everlasting love?

God was willing to send His only begotten Son to die for us. Acts 4:20, "For we cannot but speak the things which we have seen and heard." We witness to what we have seen and heard. We have seen God work in our lives in a big way. We were once worldly and selfish, but now we are concerned about working that which makes for peace and joy among our neighbors. 1 Chronicles 16:8-9 says, "Give thanks unto the LORD, call upon his name, make known his deeds among the people. Sing unto him, sing psalms unto him, talk ye of all his wondrous works." Allow praises to come out of your mouth every day to Him in the presence of others. We praise our cars, our homes, our beautiful clothes, our smart children. Why can't we praise our Father who begot us and gave us eternal life when we were on our way to eternal damnation? Don't *ever* let a day go by without saying something for

the Lord. It'll enrich your life and those around

you; but not only that, it'll also advance the very

Kingdom of God! "But ye shall receive power, after

that the Holy Ghost is come upon you: and ye shall

be witnesses unto me both in Jerusalem, and in all

Judaea, and in Samaria, and unto the uttermost part

of the earth (Acts 1:8)."

Lyrics

<u>Can't Let a Day Go By</u>

(Led By: Dr. Joyce Taylor)

*Can't let a day go by without saying
Something for the Lord (repeat)*

*For he is the source
of my health and strength each day
And without him I would falter and stray, away*

*Can't let a day go by without saying
Something for the Lord*

*He holds me fast (When I would go astray)
He holds my hand (And comforts me each day)
He fills me up (When I'm really feeling low)
He guides my feet (When I don't know just where to
go)*

*That's why I say he is good, he is good
He's good, he's good to me*

6

He Is the One - 1975

Philippians 2:9-11 says, "For this reason God raised him to the highest place above and gave him the name that is greater than any other name. And so, in honor of the name of Jesus all beings in heaven, on earth, and in the world below will fall on their knees, and all will openly proclaim that Jesus Christ is Lord, to the glory of God the Father."

It is projected that approximately 7 billion people inhabit earth. It's safe to say that billions of men have been born into the world, but there has not been any equal or comparable to Jesus Christ. He is in a class all by Himself. He is the greatest, the highest, the mightiest and the best. He can do more than anyone else simply because He is the Son of the living God. He is the one who lived, died, was buried, rose again and will live forevermore (Revelations 1:18). I can go on and on about Jesus' eminence and his greatness.

John 1:3 says, "All things were made by him; and without him was not anything made that was made." Now would you think of that? Every single thing that's in existence is because of Him; and without Him there would be nothing. As a matter of fact, without Him we can do nothing and can't make it through anything.

He can lift your burden no matter how heavy it may be. He can change your circumstances, no matter how sad they may be. He can build your confidence, no matter how shaky it may be. He's able to open your understanding in any and every area that is needed. He gives seed to the sower. He heals the sick. He can even open doors that absolutely no man can shut. The more I meditate upon Him, the more I realize that I need Him. Jesus, who washed away my sins and redeemed my soul from hell. He gave me blessed assurance. He lifted me up out of despair and clothed me with His righteousness. I don't have to rely on my own righteousness which is as filthy rags (Isaiah 64:6).

It amazes me how many people have denied Jesus for one reason or another. To deny Christ is to never know life. I recommend you look to Him for companionship and victorious living, for everyday contentment, and daily blessings. He's the one to look to for miraculous signs, wonders and confirmations of His Word. To deny Christ is to never know life.

All kinds of power exist in our world: man power, electrical power, political power, financial, demonic, psychic, wind and water power, solar and nuclear power, but Jesus has *ALL POWER*. Do you know what that means? That means Christ has the power over all those that I've mentioned and even those not known by man. Luke 10:19 19 says, "Behold, I give unto you power to tread on serpents and scorpions, and over all the power of the enemy: and nothing shall by any means hurt you." Listen, we have power because Jesus gave it to us. It's all we need. It's power *OVER ALL THE POWER OF THE ENEMY*. You don't need any more than that.

We need to be able to shut down the enemy from ruling in our business. We can do just that because The Lord gave us power to do so. See, when you know Him and when you've developed a relationship with Him you know who He is in you.

I wrote a song, years ago, entitled *He Is the One*. Back then wasn't too different from now. In every generation, you can always find a group of folks who will deny Christ and cast off His power and importance. I wrote this song in hopes that it travels down through generations and serve as a reminder that Jesus Christ is *THE ONE*! He is *THE WAY*! He is *THE TRUTH*! And He certainly is *THE LIFE*! I've lived long enough to know my dear friends that you can't live without Him. And I dare not try. See, it is pride that lives in the man or woman's heart that thinks they can do it alone. It's even worse for those who think they can lean and depend on people. Let me tell you, men and women will let you down. I've reckoned that you'll even let yourself down. Just keep right on living. There's nothing and no one who is as consistent, strong, and righteous as Jesus Christ. As a matter of fact, we are made righteous through Him. That's the only way we can manifest the fruits of righteousness. Once we receive Christ, he gives us the power to live right. Paul said, "In my flesh dwells no good thing (Romans 7:18)." Without Christ we are slaves to our flesh, but with Christ we are birthed into a victorious life. Oh, rest assured there is a power that lives down on the inside of us. But you can't tap into it by yourself, you can't steward it properly and you can't use it appropriately unless you follow the teachings of Christ and allow His Holy Spirit to be your guide.

Christ bestowed power first upon His Disciples. Luke 9:1-2 records, "Then he called his twelve disciples together, and gave them power and authority over all devils, and to cure diseases. And he sent them to preach the kingdom of God, and to heal the sick." Oh my goodness! Did you hear that? Read this scripture out loud. Luke 9:1-2 says, "Then he called his twelve disciples together, and gave them power and authority over all devils, and to cure diseases. And he sent them to preach the kingdom of God, and to heal the sick." *YES!* So, you know what that means? Now that we are disciples of Jesus Christ too; we can have that same power. But it is manifested through the Spirit of Christ working with us (Mark 16:20).

Now, I know that doctrine is a bit old school, but I still very much believe it to be true. I would truly be remiss if I would close this chapter without reminding all who read it that He is the only one by which we must be saved. Salvation is in no other. John 14:6 says, "Jesus saith unto him, I am the way, the truth, and the life: no man cometh unto the Father, but by me. Jesus is the only one who bridged the gap between God and man. *THE ONLY ONE.* Had it not been for His great sacrifice on the cross at Golgotha there would be no reconciliation. No reconciliation, no salvation. No salvation, no eternal life with the Father.

Acts 4:12 speaks clearly and reminds us that, "Neither is there salvation in any other: *(He is the only one)* for there is none other name under heaven given among men, whereby we must be saved." *NO OTHER!* He is the way the *ONLY WAY.* Salvation is a package deal. It's not just fire insurance, but promises are made to us if we keep His commandments. *NO GOOD THING WILL HE WITHHOLD* from those who walk upright before Him. Isn't that awesome?

We are assigned to do business as authorized representatives of our Lord until He returns. We are told that it is the Father's good pleasure to give us the Kingdom.

This is the answer to a question that millions have asked and I'm sure millions will ask. Is there anyone who can help me with the trials of life, with the struggles of finding comfort for my soul? Paul among many others asked this question in Romans 7:24. And there are a number of other scripture references to assure you that yes, there is someone and His name is Jesus (2 Corinthians 1:10: Galatians 1:4; 2 Timothy 4:18; 2 Peter 2:9; and Hebrews 2:15.)

We must last through hard trials. We must be strong through disappointments. The only way to do that is to be anchored in Jesus. He is the only one who can hold you fast. He is The Living Word. The word has the power to keep, hold, anchor, sooth, comfort and so much more. Immersion into His Word will get you over and through anything. Yes, there is one!

Don't ever stop believing in Him. Even in these modern times where it seems that our culture has made Christianity and the belief in Christ a backseat sport, you keep right on trusting in Him. Even though in many churches and multiple people's lives it seems that worship is taboo or even strange, you keep right on worshiping and praising Him like the Bible instructs. Don't ever allow your love for Christ to become stagnant or cold, because He is the only one. If your faith is not in Him alone, then you might as well not have any faith at all. There is no other. So, go ahead and lean on Him. Rely upon His Word. Use your authority given by Him. Enjoy His awesome love. Trust in His mercy and His amazing grace. Follow in His footsteps. The assurance of who He is will overtake you. All doubts will be settled.

He is the one in whom my soul takes great delight, to whom I lift my hands and my voice. He is the one I bow my knees to; unto whom I sing praises. I give Him my all. I will never be able to lift Him high enough, praise Him long enough, or serve Him well enough. Yet, I will spend the rest of my days giving Him all that I am. I am persuaded that *HE IS THE ONE.*

HE IS THE ONE, THE ONLY ONE. Remember this.

He's the One

(Led by Rubenstien McClure)

Is there anyone
Who understands our hearts
When the storms of life
Has pierced them till they bleed
One who is all aware
And will our burdens share
I know of no other
No one but Jesus

Is there anyone
Who can dispel our doubts
When we care to stand and fall away
God who can hold us fast
And make us thru hard trials last
I know of no other
no one but Jesus

There is one
There is only one
His name is Jesus

Sweet, Merciful Jesus

When afflictions press my soul
And the weight of trials fall
When sinful habits will gave your soul bound
And it seems there's no solution around
And when it seems my faith will fail
And the tempter will prevail

He is the one
The only one
No one but Jesus

7

Satisfied with Jesus - 1974

In my opinion, a lot of Sermons today really focus on the flesh. What I mean by that is they make us more aware of our flesh *(body and soul)* than they do our spirit. Our spirit man needs to be built up and strengthened so that we can face life with the right attitude. We live in this world, but we are not of this world. We are to train our bodies to respond to our renewed spirit and not to our corruptible flesh. Reckoning our flesh to be dead. You owe the flesh nothing, yet we pay more attention to it than we do to the eternal spirit. If you ask me, this is why so many people are tossed here, there, and everywhere when it comes to life's demands and stressors. It's because their spirit has not been fed long enough to conquer and override the things in and of the flesh when a problem arises.

And while so many keep their attention on the flesh, it's sad to say that I don't think that your flesh will ever be satisfied. But our spirit certainly can be, if we build it up on the Word of God. Here's my point, we must feed the spirit daily and it will become strong. Stronger than your flesh.

People are often not satisfied because their goals are not met, dreams are not realized, plans have not come together, so on and so on. Their dissatisfaction will often show on their faces or come out in their speech; even slow down their movement and progression.

It's important to be satisfied in life and you *can* have a sense of satisfaction even while your goals are being worked on and your dreams are in the process of being developed. I'm not surprised that the world does not know this but surely the Church, The Body of Christ should.

We know that Jesus satisfies. Everything that we could possibly want or need Jesus have already provided.

Satisfaction brings joy. Just like faith brings Joy. When you are in faith it means that you have received what you asked for even though you don't see it physically. If you have (believed) received your promises fulfilled, your questions answered your burdens rolled away then you should be satisfied. You can have satisfaction and contentment in knowing that God has already worked out and established your tomorrow if you're engulfed in Him and His word. All that you need and desire—according to the will of God—are supplied by Him according to 2 Peter 1:3. Jesus is the Lord of your life. There is a certain comfort that comes with that.

As I've lived this life, I've found that many don't know what true satisfaction and contentment looks like. Simply put, if you are satisfied you are not worried. You are not sad or depressed as one with no hope. You know when a person is happy and when they are sad. You can tell when a person is unhappy or when they're filled with the joy of the Lord. Happy people smile, laugh, sing, make joyful noises. They are enjoying life. Now, that doesn't mean that life doesn't happen. That simply means that they don't get stuck in the curves and bends of life. They don't run off the road at every turn. But they take on life full throttle with confidence. They go with God. And when they go with God they will make it.

If you are truly a part of the Body of Christ you should be satisfied with Jesus and in Jesus. Why? Colossians 2:9 says, "For in him *(Jesus)* dwelleth all the fullness of the Godhead bodily." Wow! Did you read that? If you are engrafted in Jesus and the Word of God, you have access to all that the Godhead is. Not that we are God or gods. But that we can experience the Father, Son and Holy Spirit (John 14:23, Ephesians 4:15, and 2 Peter 1:4). Who could ask for anything more? That's absolutely amazing! How could you be sad? How could you be overcome with depression? Now, I know what you're saying. "Well Bishop, sadness and depression are just a part of life. Everybody deals with it from time to time." I'm not saying you won't experience these things for a moment, just like Jesus Christ did on the mount after his fast. But tell the enemy and whoever else will listen what is written, and you will come out victoriously. Like I said, you may go there for a moment but don't stay there: you don't have to.

If God gave up His Son to die on the cross for you, how much more won't He freely give you all things (Romans 8:32)? What else can God give? If that doesn't satisfy you then you are rejecting His help. Salvation is not just escaping hell, but it's also assurance of all the promises of God to His obedient children.

At the time that I wrote this song *Satisfied with Jesus* I have to admit I was not as knowledgeable of the scriptures as I am today. But let me hasten to say I am not as knowledgeable of the scriptures today as I will be in the future. At that time, I knew what I was experiencing in Him, but what it all meant not so much. I've learned more, and I'm still learning. See the joy of the Lord is our strength and we are to be strong. The strong spirit of a man will sustain him in trouble. I don't understand the joy of the Lord totally, but it has been revealed to me that a glad heart is a receptive heart. My Uncle Jasper used to say, "The Lord comes on a glad heart." Jesus would say to those seeking healing, "Be of good cheer," before He would minister to them. Why? Because gladness denotes faith. And faith brings the answer, the help. You are happy when you know you have what you ask for, that's what faith is.

What I've learned over the years is that the joy of the Lord causes us to jump up, spin around in a dance, shout and scream no matter what you are experiencing or facing. My cousin Fanny would say, "J.C. whenever the devil tells you to sit down, jump up! When we rejoice we directly oppose the enemy.

Listen my friend, when things are not going well with you, when sorrow floods the atmosphere there is a peace and a joy that I've found in Jesus Christ. Even when I mess up, I still have joy. Did you hear me? Yes, I'm not always making righteous decisions. I'm not always walking in the perfected love of God, but that still doesn't mean I can't have the joy of the Lord. Why? Because I don't walk in condemnation anymore since I met Jesus. See, back then—and even now—I knew that He gave me that kind of joy. I would have run away in shame and sorrow. But even in my broken state, there was still reason to praise Him. Even though I thought I had disappointed Him. I just couldn't be in a service and not say, "Thank you Jesus, God you're good, or I love you Lord." As I think about it,

My soul is even now saying, "Hallelujah!" Ha! I just can't stop having joy. The joy of the Lord is infectious and repetitive.

Another gift God gave me is love. He gave me love for my neighbor, love for my brothers and sisters in Christ, and yes even love for myself. Before He came into my life I loved with conditions, but because He came into my life I loved effortlessly and generously. I realized that's just the way He loves me. He loved me and I was undeserving. Andre Crouch used to sing, "I don't know why He loved me. I don't know why He cared. I don't know why He sacrificed His life. Oh, but I'm glad, so glad He did." See, love for others came into my heart. I could love because *HE SHED HIS LOVE* abroad in *MY HEART* by the Holy Ghost. With God I've been experiencing and administering agape love.

I always say that love has everything to do with everything. It's impossible to please God without faith; according to Hebrew 11:6. "For without faith it is impossible to please him: for he that cometh to God must believe that he is, and that he is a rewarder of them that diligently seek him." But let's be clear, Faith works by *LOVE*; according to Galatians 5:6. It says, "For in Jesus Christ neither circumcision availeth anything, nor uncircumcision; but faith which worketh by love." 1 Corinthians 13:13 says, "And now abideth faith, hope, charity, these three; but the greatest of these is charity, which is interpreted love."

Jesus Christ is a comfort to my soul. Our souls sometimes get wounded along the way. There are things that happened in life that may have hurt you, things that were said that stunned you. There may be things that occurred that made you feel less than. I hear stories all the time about abuse and neglect by family members, as well as strangers. Let me tell you, Christ healed your soul when He made you whole. You just have to walk in it. Receive the healing. Receive the wholeness. A healed soul is not still crying over the pass, but it is rejoicing in the newness of life.

You can be satisfied with Jesus alone because He is your provider and source for everything. A person should be satisfied when he/she have all that they need and want, right? This is exactly what the love of Christ feels like. Even though you may not tangibly have it all yet, you're still joyful and satisfied in your soul and your spirit. Why? Because you know that in Christ Jesus you have all sufficiency; and there's absolutely nothing you will go lacking for as you live. If your wants and needs are in line with the word of God, then you know they are yours and it's just a matter of time before they will be manifested.

"You can live the satisfied life," says Dr. Dennis Burke. God wants you to! Don't let your spirit shrivel up and draw back. God has no pleasure in a drawback spirit. The joy of the Lord is your strength. Sing unto the Lord a new song and let one of them be, "With Jesus alone I'm satisfied."

Lyrics

Satisfied with Jesus
(Led by Maxine Jones)

You know he saved my soul from sin
And then he gave me peace within
He soothed all my doubts and fears
He dried my crying tears
He mended my broken heart
And then he gave me a brand new start
And right now I'm satisfied (Satisfied with Jesus,
repeat)

You know he gave me joy and peace
My strength he did increase
He's been a comfort to my soul
Ever since he's made me whole
I praise the Lord the most
For the gift of the Holy Ghost
And right now I'm satisfied (Satisfied with Jesus,
repeat)

Satisfied (repeat)
With Jesus alone, I'm satisfied

Gave me joy sublime

Gave me love divine and I'm satisfied

Saved me, raised me, lifts me up and I'm satisfied
He brought me, taught me, soothed me

He filled me, thrilled me, moved me
He healed me, sealed me, picked me up and I'm
satisfied

Guides me, hides me (repeat)

8

Talk It Over with Jesus - 1972

Talk it over with Jesus is just another way of saying, "Develop and keep a close relationship with Jesus. Consult Him in everything you do. Don't let a day go by without acknowledging His infinite wisdom, power, and grace." Romans 12:12 says, "Pray about everything." Every day you should be rejoicing in the hope of Christ. Why? Because the same power that's in Jesus Christ resides in you; causing you to be patient in tribulation, consistent in prayer, consistent in devotion unto Him.

Having a persistent and steadfast relationship with God and possessing the power of Christ through tenacious prayer compels you to be steadfastly attentive unto His word, it gives you the power to have unremitting care for others and the things of God, and it also allows you to persevere and not to faint in the midst of hard times. We can see from Romans 12:12 that the Apostle Paul wanted the Roman Church to know that prayer was to be a constant part of their walk in this Christian race.

Ephesians 6:18 declares, "Praying always with all prayer and supplication in the Spirit and watching thereunto with all perseverance and supplication for all saints; praying always with all prayer and supplication in the spirit." A part of the armor that we are to put on each day before we go out into the mission fields of life is prayer. Prayer is a weapon, a tool to be used in Christian warfare. It is powerful. Because the scriptures said that, Whatsoever we ask in prayer believing we shall have it." Did you hear that? *WHATSOEVER* you ask in prayer. Now, let's be clear. This is why you must have a strong connection and relationship with God Almighty. It is very possible to pray amiss or to pray the wrong prayers. You can very much so call things into your life and into existence that are not supposed to be so; but because of the principle of prayer it's very possible for things outside of God's will to manifest in your life. This is why we must stick close to the heart of God, so that we might know the will of God. You're supposed to always pray the will of God, not necessarily your own agenda. When you come into direct communion with Christ, your desires should automatically become His desires.

Now, over the years I've learned that there are different kinds of prayer and it would be to our advantage to know what kind of prayer should be prayed according to our needs, desires and situations. There are such things as warfare prayers, prayers of thanksgiving and gratitude, prayers of supplication and petition, prayers of declaration, affirmations, and legislations. There are all types of prayers. Prayer comes in all shapes and forms. And you must be privy to what they are. I certainly do not have much time to dive into all of them and explain in totality what they are. That's, perhaps, another book too. But ask God by His Holy Spirit to lead and guide you in His word; and to open you up to the revelation of knowing the different levels, dimensions, components, and types of prayer. Not being ignorant of these things will help you pray the right thing at the right times; even usurp the authority of ill-intended prayers that may have been relegated into your life.

We know that we are to pray to the Father in the name of Jesus; and no other spiritual or physical force. If it were not for Jesus we would not have any right to say anything to the Father, but because of Jesus we can come boldly to the throne of God our Father. And yes, He hears us.

Talking things over with Jesus to me is actually searching the scriptures to see what the Word *(which is a culmination of who Jesus is)* has to say about you, your life, or your concern. That's why I wrote the song, *Talking It Over with Jesus.* " I wanted men and women all over the world to know that they too can talk it over with Jesus. Many people are losing the battle of life because they do not perceive that they have enough power or influence to pray a thing and it be established. My dear friends, here's why you must read the scriptures. You don't know who you really are in Christ Jesus. If so, you'd know that the scripture tells us time and time again how we have authority, power, and influence even in the spiritual realm when we pray. You can only access and strengthen that power by communicating and talking with the spirit of Christ *(which is the Holy Spirit)* every day.

Jesus--the Living Word—is your light and revelation on anything that you want to know. You must have light, understanding, and revelation knowledge on a subject before you pray about it. You can't ask, seek, or knock on the door and expect an answer for anything or situation unless first you have revelation of the principles of what you're praying for. You might be in a situation where all you have time to say is Lord save me like Peter when he was going down. And at that moment that's all you really need to say. But you can be much more effective and influential in the spirit realm when you study the word of God commune and sup with Christ by way of His spirit and build a constant internal dialogue with God. If you've done this you can move many more mountains in the spirit, unlock greater doors of blessing, portals of revelation, and so forth. My friends, if you haven't already, you've got to get in the habit of opening God's word every day. When you do this, you are preparing yourself for whatever comes. You will not have to be tossed to and fro, here and there and everywhere. But rather, you will be steadfast and unmovable. You will be rooted and planted like that tree in Psalm 1 that was planted by the rivers of living water.

Let me encourage your heart and remind you. When you are in doubt, wonder, or despair; talk it over with Jesus. Go to the Word of God, seek godly Council. Immerse yourself in the principles that you've already learned through your constant relationship with Christ. Then declare what you've learned. That's how you get the victory every time.

You can't be passive with your prayer life and your relationship with God anymore.

Surely Jesus knows all about your struggles. He was tempted in all points. Hebrews 4:15-16 establishes, "For we have not an high priest which cannot be touched with the feeling of our infirmities; but was in all points tempted like as [we are, yet] without sin. Let us therefore come boldly unto the throne of grace, that we may obtain mercy, and find grace to help in time of need." Wait a minute. Did you see that my brothers and sisters? The latter part of this scripture says, "Let us therefore come boldly unto the throne of grace, that we may obtain mercy, and find grace to help in time of need." Brothers and sisters, talking it over with Jesus isn't always easy when you're in time of need.

I won't sit here and act like it is. But there's a grace for it. Grace—at its simplest form—means supernatural ability. That means you have an ability to do something that's beyond your limited, finite, fleshly self. It's an ability that's beyond you. You couldn't even explain it if you wanted to. Somehow—by the spirit of the living God—you can pray and declare a thing and it be established on earth as it already is in heaven. That's not you. That's your grace working for you; empowering you on how to pray according to the word and principles you've been studying.

Hebrews 2:18 declares, "For in that he himself hath suffered being tempted, he is able to succor *(or help)* them that are tempted." Listen, whatever you want to talk about He is already familiar with.

God's already got the answer before the question was even asked. To say He will work it out is to say He will show you the path to your victory. Many times, in the Old Testament God told His people to go and possess. He said, "Go," because He had already given them the victory. But in order to see what God said they had to inquire of him and then do what He said step-by-step. You do this through prayer *(having a little talk with Jesus).* The victory was in whatever He told them to do; and if they obeyed they saw the victory. Today God have given us His Word and what He wants *(His will)* is outlined in there. There are times though when He might speak to you directly in a still small voice or an unction by the Holy Spirit. Either way you must learn and train your 5 senses, your mind, and your spirit to know His voice and follow his lead. This entails knowing His Word. He will never tell you anything that is against His Word. That's exactly how you know it's Him that's speaking.

Trust and know that often times God will work things out for you as you go. As you go He will set ambushments for your enemy. He will cause walls to fall, He will frighten the enemy and cause confusion among them. He will work on your behalf. He will cause angels to be on post and guard to usher you out of the prison. He will allow natural disasters to occur just to get you out. God will orchestrate and strategically work it out on your behalf every time! So, when in doubt, when in despair, anytime, anywhere. Talk it over and give it over to Jesus.

If you haven't already, you've got to get in the habit of opening God's word every day. When you do this, you are preparing yourself for whatever comes. You will not have to be tossed to and fro, here and there and everywhere. But rather, you will be steadfast and unmovable. You will be rooted and planted like that tree in Jeremiah 17:8 For he shall be as a tree planted by the waters, and *that* spreadeth out her roots by the river, and shall not see when heat cometh, but her leaf shall be green; and shall not be careful in the year of drought, neither shall cease from yielding fruit. You will flourish.

The Bible says that we should not be careful (full of care) about anything but in all things, pray........... Be careful for nothing; but in

everything by prayer and supplication with
thanksgiving let your requests be made known unto
God. "And the peace of God, which passeth all
understanding, shall keep your hearts and minds
through Christ Jesus."

Let me encourage your heart and remind
you. When you are in doubt, in despair, anytime
anywhere talk it over with Jesus. Jessie Duplantis
says he sometimes just talk to the Lord like he
would talk to any friend. He says things like, "Good
morning Lord what do you want me to do today,"
and God might even ask him, "What do you want to
do today Jessie?" Ha!

Surely Jesus knows all about your struggles.
He was tempted in all points. Hebrews 4:15-16
establishes, "For we have not an high priest which

cannot be touched with the feeling of our infirmities; but was in all points tempted like as [we are, yet] without sin. Let us therefore come boldly unto the throne of grace, that we may obtain mercy, and find grace to help in time of need." Wait a minute. Did you see that my brothers and sisters? The latter part of this scripture says, "Let us therefore come boldly unto the throne of grace, that we may obtain mercy, *and find grace to help in time of need.*" My brothers and sisters, talking it over with Jesus is the best move you can make because you can find no other who knows what to do about any and every situation. Hardship, pain, a loss, loneliness any decision to be made or any burden weighing you down, just give it to Jesus.

To some this might seem sacrilegious, but I thought about the fact that sometimes I pray without using all the religious jargon. It might be something like Lord I don't know what to do, please show me or Lord help me, like Peter did when he was drowning. The point is the Lord heard him, and guess what He hears me. I'm giving you this example because I want you to know that when you are coming against organized forces and you know the proper protocol for waring in the spirit until strongholds are broken then you should do so. but there are also times when you need to ask and receive on the spot. Plus, you need to act like Jesus is with you always and knows and sees everything. He is in you as a matter of fact so talk to Him anytime you want to or need to.

Lyrics

Talk it over with Jesus

(Led by Mother Rubenstein McClure and Evang. Regina Key)

When your burdens seem hard to bear
And so bitter the lot you share

When in doubt, in despair
Anytime, anywhere
Talk it over with Jesus

If in sorrow you're bound today
God will wipe every one of your tears away

When in doubt, in despair
Anytime, anywhere
Talk it over with Jesus

If you're working for the master down here
And you're having so many doubts and fears

When in doubt, in despair
Anytime, anywhere
Talk it over with Jesus

Find out you don't have a friend

To stand by you to the end
Can't seem to find your way
binding you night and day

When in doubt, in despair

Anytime, anywhere

Talk it over with Jesus

He'll work it out!

9

New Life in Christ - 1981

Certainly, before we gave our life to Christ we were burdened and heavy laden with sin. Now you might not want to admit it, but it's true. We were doomed, on our way to eternal damnation. We were living, but lifeless. Sin is transgression of the law of God. Where there is transgression of a law there is a penalty to be paid. That penalty was going to be our life before we gave it over to Christ to save.

If you are the transgressor you know that you are liable to be caught and demanded to pay whatever is demanded. Adam transgressed the law of God and the price to be paid was the shedding of blood. It couldn't be Adam's blood because Adam was the one who sinned. Thank God for *Jesus (the second Adam)*, the sinless one, who paid the price. But unless you believe this and accept and walk in this truth then the price is still yours to pay. And because you cannot pay it, the only way to escape the penalty is to accept and receive Jesus Christ. Accepting the shed blood of Jesus Christ gets you off the hook. When you realize, you are off the hook you have reason to rejoice, sing, shout, dance and testify about it. You rejoice because of the revelation that you have a new life in Christ; a new love that's everlasting. God's Word speaks of giving us a new spirit, a new heart, a renewed mind, a new song, and even a new name.

Revelation 21:1 announces, "I saw a new heaven and a new earth: for the first heaven and the first earth were passed away; and there was no more sea." Wow. Would you look at that! A new heaven and a new earth is being prepared for a new people. We who have put off the old man are made a new nation. One that never existed before. God puts new with new. Old wine skins are not fit to hold new wine. John 13:34 also says, "A new commandment I give unto you, that ye love one another; as I have loved you, that ye also love one another." Wow a new commandment! He gave us a new commandment. God told the people to keep His commandment and live. The new commandment of love brings forth life in our spirits, our minds, and our bodies. The Old Testament gave the Israelites, God's people, commandments to live by. There were over 600 of them. God's people were to keep them and if they did they would escape the penalty of breaking them which was ultimately death. It was too much for them they couldn't do it in their own natural power and ability. God knew they couldn't, but they wanted to do in the flesh what could only be done in the spirit. They failed of course. And don't you know that God knew this would happen. My God was proving a point. But when the time had fully come Jesus the Lamb of God came into the world to save sinners once and for all. He announced to His followers in John 13:34, "A new commandment I give unto you, that ye love one another; as I have loved you, that ye also love one another. By this shall all men know that ye are my disciples, if ye have love one to another." We are recognized as His Disciples by the love that we have for one another. I guess that clears up a lot of different churches and denominations' actions. To act any other way but in love proves that you are not God's disciples. Even if you say you are.

God is into NEW. He likes it and so do I. After a while things get old and when they do many times they don't function the way they used to. Most often a new thing will come out that has more capability than the old. Sometimes the old thing will not look presentable, so we will often get a new one. God went to great extent to make us new. Born in sin was not the best that we could be. So, Jesus came preaching the kingdom and telling us that in order to come into it we must be born again. Born of the Spirit because that which is born of the flesh is flesh; and the flesh is weak, lustful, and fights to have its own way. Being born of the Spirit is submitting to the Spirit of God and allowing Him to produce His spirit and power within you.

We are human whether we are saved or not but we are not our best until we have received Jesus into our lives. God welcomes us into the kingdom *(His Kingdom)* and makes us new.

This particular song, *New Life New Love,* was written in order to express the joy of experiencing the new life and love that is ours now that we are living in Christ Jesus. It's a life that's so much better than before. New things make you feel fresh and confident. They make you happy. If this is true with material things; then how much more will the new life and love that Christ gives you make you happy. Your new life, the life that came from accepting Jesus as Lord and Savior is so much higher and better than the old life of sin. The sinful life robbed you of joy, peace and happiness in the earth and offers you death and destruction at the end of it all. Who wants that? When you are released from that sentence of doom, you will rejoice and thank God for your new life.

New love is also ours. This love is indeed new to us. We've never known a love quite like God's before. It's so forgiving, full of grace, power, and mercy. My God. If you've never experienced the love of Christ, then you're absolutely missing life. In most cases, we have never had anyone to love us unconditionally or everlastingly; where we did not have to do anything to merit the love. The scripture says, "While we were against God He gave His Only Son to die for us." My Lord! His love for us caused Him to give up what He had only one of; even when we turned our backs on Him as a human race. His love for us is everlasting, we can't pin point a starting place because He loved us even before the foundation of the world and it will never end. Oh, my brothers and sisters, I love Him because He first loved me.

We would not know real love had not we been shown it by what God through Christ Jesus did for us. John 3:16-17 shows us, "For God so loved the world, that he gave his only begotten Son, that whosoever believeth in him should not perish, but have everlasting life." I'm so grateful for the given Son! That scripture goes on to say, "For God sent not his Son into the world to condemn the world;

but that the world through him might be saved." Some of us got it all wrong for too long. Our job is to lift up the name of Jesus by showing the love of Christ. The new commandment is love. Love will push you and force you into a higher state and on a better plane of living. Love will call you out of the low places and tell you who you really are. Love will say, "You're better than that." Love will give you hope for tomorrow, joy for your sorrow. I'm talking about God's love.

Now we know that love is what love does. 1 Corinthians 13:4-7 says, "We know that love suffereth long, and is kind; love envieth not; love vaunteth not itself, is not puffed up, doth not behave itself unseemly, seeketh not her own, is not easily provoked, thinketh no evil; rejoiceth not in iniquity, but rejoiceth in the truth; beareth all things, believeth all things, hopeth all things, and endureth all things." These are God's actions and attitude towards us. Furthermore, this should be our actions and attitude towards each other. This is the new love that I have come into. The Old love was conditional. "I love you because you meet my needs, you give me what I want, but if you kick my dog I'll kick your cat." It was a tit for tat love, a quid pro quo kind of love as they'd say in the Corporate arena. But now that God has showed us how to love without cause; I encourage you to love in spite of.

God loves us when we are good and when we are bad. Even when we are chastened He does it because He loves us. "We had fathers who chastened us after their own pleasure; but He for our profit, that we might be partakers of his holiness. He's a good good Father who, if we trust in Him, He gives us richly all things to enjoy," according to 1 Timothy 6:17b. God gives us things to enjoy. Some might be surprised at that, but God loves us and wants us to enjoy our lives here on earth. A part of what makes us joyful and glad should be showing Him and our fellow man love in return. I believe this gives God good pleasure to hear us speak and sing of His goodness. Not that He is egotistical, but because He knows when we do this our faith is strengthened. And when our faith is strong, our confidence is high, and we will ask what we will and He will do it. With God, it's all about us. With us it should be all about Him. Now that's what you call a loving relationship!

We can have new life and new love that fills us with joy; joy unspeakable and full of glory. Redemption is a form of extravagant love. Love that goes beyond the call of duty. Now that's something new! Redeemed means when one does something to compensate for poor behavior. It was love that caused the Lord to pay for our sins. And it was not for our praise, because He had all of Heaven to praise Him. It was because of His love for humanity; His creation. He so loved us that He gave His only begotten Son. The Bible did not say, "God so wanted praise, or God so need our validation that He gave His only Son." NO! It said, "God so *loved*." And guess what? He will not allow anything to separate us from His love. This means that nothing can get Him to stop loving us. Now THAT'S NEW! When you're dealing with your family or friends, you just might do something that makes them stop loving you. But this isn't so with God. I've received that agape love. Have you? It's new and different from that of the world. Not only did God give us peace that the world does not give, but He also gave us love that the world does not give. The new love that I have is the same as God has. That's the new love that we sing about. This has not always been my testimony but the old is passed away, behold all things have become new. All things are new because of my new life in Christ.

Lyrics

New Life, New Love

Verse: Hear the story now, let me tell you how

I've got a (New life, new love)

It's the grandest thing, how my heart does sing

I've got a (New life, new love)

It's so grand and true, and it can be for you

I've got a (New life, new love)

If you do not know, I'm here to tell you so

I've got a (New life, new love)

Vamp: I heard the voice of Jesus say

Come unto me and (Rest)

Lay down thy weary one

Lay down thy head upon me (Breast)

I listen to his tender call

Or how my soul's been blessed

My soul's been blessed!

Drive: I've got a new life in Christ

New love, everlasting

10

A Little More Grace - 1968

I vividly remember the occasion when I asked the Lord for _a little more grace._ In the late 60's, I was in Texas attending the Youth Congress of the Churches of God In Christ. I had a contract with United Artists to write songs for some singing groups that were signed for the new gospel wing of the company headed by Mr. George Butler. He had the singers; but they needed the songs. As I stated in the Introduction of this book, I took my song book with me. At the time I was just writing up a storm. Songs would just come to me effortlessly. As I attended the conference in Texas, I continued writing songs to present to the label for the artists. I had already written some great ones before the conference, and the songs just kept flowing. I can remember it like it was yesterday. I skipped some of the activities of the Congress and stayed in my room to write.

Then finally we came to the end of the conference that week. It was the last day of the Congress and we had choir rehearsal. I took my briefcase with me with my songbook in it to the rehearsal. I put it under my seat in the choir stand; and it stayed there all evening through the night service. I left the service forgetting that it was there under the seat. And I didn't remember the briefcase until the next morning. When I went back to the auditorium to get it, it was not there. I was stunned!

I was so speechless. I could not believe that anyone would steal my suitcase. After all, this was a church event? Didn't they know how valuable this thing was? Didn't they understand that God had opened a major door for me to write songs for a major label? How could someone be so insensitive?

As I stood there in the auditorium stunned in disbelief and mute I realized that we were running late; and I had to rush to the airport to return home. I felt so sick. I felt like a piece of me had died. These songs meant so much to me. It wasn't just because of the opportunity; but these songs were the contents of my heart. Ever since I could remember, all I've ever wanted to do was convey God's love and His will to the masses through song. Everything that God was to me, everything that He's done for me. This was placed in the words of these songs. As I got on the airplane I just couldn't get myself together. I mean to think, I had to leave without my briefcase.

See if you haven't noticed by now, my briefcase was more than just filled with songs for a label. It was filled with my heart, my passion, my destiny. Everything that God made me was locked away in briefcase. Words that I hoped would change the lives of many, were lost in that case. When I arrived home, I remembered that Kitty Parham, the Director of the choir, was remaining there in the hotel so I called her. She had recovered my briefcase. Thank the Lord! She told me that the group that she sings with was going to be at the Apollo in Harlem that weekend and she would bring it with her. My heart rejoiced! I was so glad! That following Sunday morning my pastor, Bishop Carl E. Williams Sr., preached about grace. That was God speaking directly to me. I just knew it. I still know it to this day.

I went up to Harlem to the Apollo Theatre that Sunday evening. I got in touch with Kitty Parham who was backstage preparing for her show; only to find out that the briefcase had been indeed stolen out of her car. Of course, I was devastated. I can remember crying as I went up and down the block looking in garbage cans. Sadness turned into anger. Anger, after a while, turned in to hyperventilation. I mean, I was so angry and upset that I could hardly catch my breath. See, again, you've got to realize that this wasn't just a briefcase with songs. But these were songs from my heart. These were songs whose messages were straight from God. They touched my life; and I was going to share them with the world. I can remember as I walked up and down that Harlem sidewalk saying, "God, I just need a little more grace. I need *YOUR* grace." I prayed, "Lord let whoever took it see that there is nothing of value to them in it and tossed it in a garbage can." But it wasn't to be.

After that event, for a long while, I lost my ability to hear anything in the way of a song. I couldn't write anything. I tried and tried; but I could not hear or sense anything. I was numb. That moment of loss had taken my breath away. Any songwriter or artist knows the feeling. I was perplexed because my motives were pure. My intent was to encourage the saints and help the lost to find their way to the Savior. So how could this happen? It's debilitating. Not only was I unable to produce songs for a while. On top of that, I lost my job with United Artists. I thought I would never write again. But I found out Jesus gives us more grace each time we need it. His grace has brought many, including me, through the veil of tears and nights of despair.

In James 4:6 the Bible says, "But he gives more grace, wherefore he resists the proud; but gives grace the humble." Ephesians 4:7 says, "But unto every one of us is given grace, according to the measure of the gift of Christ." 1 Timothy 1:14 says, "The grace of our Lord was exceeding abundant [or plenteous] with faith and love which is in Christ." His grace is often revealed in various ways. He allows us to live another day, grants us another opportunity, sees us through circumstances, gives us strength equal to our task and wisdom for our problems. Grace comes in many different forms.

I got through that harsh period in my life; and because of his grace I later wrote the song *A Little More Grace*. When the world hears the word *grace* they may think of things that are graceful, elegant, charming or beautiful in the natural. But when believers talk about grace we mean something more significant. God is completely Holy and without sin. He requires that we also be Holy. However, we all are sinners and can never meet his perfect standard, but God is a God of grace and that changes everything.

Grace is also the supernatural ability to do something. When I lost my briefcase I needed the supernatural ability to beat depression, anger, guilt, and so many more emotions. All of us need God's supernatural ability and power to work in us. How do you think people beat cancer? How do you think people heal from molestation or a rape; or even a loss of a loved one? Grace is so much more than the natural mind can even comprehend in its totality. It was Grace that got you up this morning. It was Grace that gives you the strength and patience to get through those long hours at work. To be honest, it was Grace that helped me get this book written and published. Sometimes in life, you don't have all of the answers. But if you have faith in God; His Grace will overshadow you and flow in your life in the most abundant way. You'll be walking in wisdom, peace, and all the other things you so desperately need to succeed.

I've prayed for years and decades to be able to write a book. The book was to detail some of the miraculous messages behind the songs I've been blessed to write and minister all over the world. But I could never seem to get this done for whatever reason or another. Sometimes it was fear. Other times it was a lack of resources or information. Most of the time, it was just timing. See, Grace matures in its time. What do I mean by that? Well, there are certain levels of Grace that you must be prepared to walk in or handle. And it's best to say that you graduate to greater levels of Grace and supernatural ability as you steward well over the level you're currently on. I must admit, I wasn't ready to release this book back then. I had to live a little, come through some things, and be ready to give the messages I wanted the world to know clearly through my writing. I don't profess to be the world's greatest and most prolific author, but what I do profess is that I did it! I was finally able to write this book and express the messages in my heart as it relates to the songs I wrote. Although, I've written many other songs these were some of the ones that was nearest and dearest to my heart.

If you don't get any other message from these songs or this book; please let this be your takeaway. God is a great God; and He loves you dearly. He will give you brand new life; and new life abundantly. If you just stick with God, He'll lead you in all truth. He'll lead you through the storms of life; into a life of victory. And just know that each day you wake up you've been given the opportunity to access just a little more Grace. These are my songs. These are my messages. And they come from my heart. They are the messages behind the melodies that have blessed hundred—perhaps millions—for decades. It is my prayer that this book will ignite a passion and a love for Christ in this new generation of believer and the believers to come.

May the words in this book and messages behind each melody I've written continue to live on for generations to come. And may they forever be a testament of my faith, my God, and my heart.

Lyrics

Little More Grace

(Led by Delores Gatewood-Phillips)

All I want right now from Jesus
(Just give me a little more grace)
That's all I need to run this race
(Oh, a little more grace)

I don't want to stop where the saints have trod
I gotta go on to see my God
(All I want is a little more grace)

I know the road to heaven
Is not a flowery bed of ease
Oh in all my striving
My savior I try to please
Satan's not going to leave me alone
To serve God as I should
That's why I'm looking for the grace God gives
Just like he said he would

(All I want from you is a little more grace)
A little more grace

Satan when you persecute me, (Grace)
Then when my lov'd ones misuse me (Grace)
Troubles on ev'ry hand (Grace)
Living in a Christian land (Grace, repeats)

Help me when the hell hounds are blazing
Keep me when the storms are raging
Hell hounds standing all around me,
Enemies camped all around me

Father and mother wont own me,
Sister and brother scorn me
All my friends misunderstand
Even tho I do all I can

Over in the midnight hour
Grace will give me power,
Oh, give it to me Jesus

About the Author

Bishop John C. White is a native of Brooklyn, New York. In his early years of ministry, he served as a Deacon at the Institutional Church of God in Christ, International and the Director of the world famous Institutional Radio Choir. His composition Stretch Out launched the Institutional Radio Choir on the road to popularity. J.C., as he is affectionately known, acknowledged his call to preach the Gospel and joined the quorum of ministers at the Institutional C.O.G.I.C., International.

In 1979, J.C., as an Elder and Assistant Pastor of the Institutional C.O.G.I.C., International was called to pastor at the Turner's Faith Temple Church of God in Christ, International in Bridgeport, Connecticut. God continually blessed the ministry under the leadership of Elder White and he was soon elevated to the office of Bishop and given the States of Connecticut and Virginia as his jurisdictions. He later served as Chairman of the Board of Bishops and Vice-Presiding Prelate. In August, 2000 he was appointed Presiding

Prelate of the Churches of God in Christ, International. Bishop White has traveled extensively throughout the United States and abroad preaching and teaching the Word of God, leading the lost to Christ and bringing the message of hope to the hopeless.

Bishop White holds an Honorary Doctorate of Sacred Music from the Pillar of Fire College in York, England for his many great musical accomplishments, a Doctorate of Divinity from the Eastern American University in Indianapolis, Indiana, and in June, 2007, Bishop White received his Doctorate of Theology from the North Carolina College of Theology.

In 2005, Bishop White established the International Bible Institute which awards graduating students with certificates in Biblical studies.

Bishop White was privileged to collaborate with Max Roach on The Fusion of Jazz and Gospel Tour which included the United States, Germany, and Spain. Bishop White served as Adjunct Professor of the Black Gospel Music Choir for Dartmouth College for many years, and he was also the first Gospel songwriter for United Artist Music Division. Bishop White is the recipient of numerous awards and trophies for songs he has written and performed around the country.

Bishop White is blessed to have songs that he wrote in the sixties and seventies still being performed today by church choirs around the world and by many notable artists such as, Vickie Winans, Latrice Pace, Judith McAllister, Ricky Dillard, Donald Lawrence, Sheri Jones-Moffett, Marvin Winans and Donnie McClurkin. The late Daryl Coley's rendition of "This is the Answer" still permeates the air waves today.

Facebook.com/glojaymusic

Dudley Publishing House

www.dphouse.net